Greyhound

Greyhound

aeon ginsberg

NOEMI PRESS

Published by Noemi Press

www.noemipress.org

Noemi Press titles are distributed to the trade by

Small Press Distribution

Phone (510) 524-1668

ISBN 978-1-934819-87-6

Cover design by Diana Arterian & Jeffrey Pethybridge

Interior design by Diana Arterian

Back cover image: "The Road Beneath the Mersey" by Terry Kearney

Printed in the United States of America

9 8 7 6 5 4 3 2 1

First edition

Noemi Press

Greyhound

FIRST THERE WAS a need to go and
no way for us to get there and so
on all fours I sprawled a body out
and on all fours a clerk calls me
she and the road is full of bodies
painted chrome and so why not
the road be femme too? Why not
call that upon which we travel
walked on? And so my voice is a stow-
away under the cabin of the buses
that take me away from myself
under my stomach where secrets pass
through me. And so first

in the terminal there is concealed
carry — but it is never what we wish
to hold in secret like a puppy or bird
or the heart of a lover upon which
the road guides us to. And first there
could have been bullets but instead
there is only my hands lathed into
dagger my mouth a wine key, the road
a drunken maiden. And there is no
on-board drinking but there are more
drivers who have seen fights happen to me
than have stopped the journey and so
first there was no way to go. And so
on all fours I sprawled spilling wine mouth
refusing to unpack my voice as it walks
out of my bod. And what I mean is

it is in a Greyhound station where I am
assumed skirt legs not pants legs and
how red my face is to not be seen pink
and gender is still a destination upon
which I leave in silence, muted, mutable.

My body a mutable gender an asphalt
paved over a pothole. Now there is a destination
and a way to travel which is my body
laid across unwelcome directions
and my gender a vehicle into which I am
not allowed on board and to say this as plainly
as I am able to.

First I entered a terminal, and was told
to be terminal. And so I left on a bus
holding a sharp dream and my life.

IN THE POEM, I try to write about dogs
but I still get ID'd wrong. Which is fair, I guess.
It costs money to get the government to stop
misidentifying you, so it's fair
that poems need to work on not misidentifying you too.

Greyhound finally accepts tickets from my phone,
but I still have to show identification.
I still have to unfurl myself and be like,
*Okay I know this is weird — this plastic calls me *******
but, to me, call me Aeon.
(To everyone else though, whatever.)

Like, yes, I get it. Trans depression means dead-name
        means flesh-prison
        means grave-soul
        means dead-end
        means one-way.

There are only two genders: depressed and correct.
In the poem where I'm a dog,
I say I'm a Chesapeake Bay retriever
and everyone says it's sad because my grandma died
and *you want to die too.*

In the poem where I leave, no one thinks it's to somewhere.

The joke in all this is the gays can't drive,
so we gotta take the bus
anyways, right?

Right.
I'm just getting on a bus
to modify this body
into something I can live in
since I can't drive to move
this body somewhere
I can live in.

I am leaving,
and a different me will return —
maybe a me who wants
to die a little less than all the time.

Even my prescriptions
have my name in parentheses.
This makes sense too — that my identity
is on the periphery of a perception of it.

I say I want to be like the dog I grew up with,
but really I want be slimmer.

A five-foot-two dog with a pixie cut
and a smaller, rounder face.
Be a manic pixie dream mutt.

Be a dog that is happy, and has a home
that they stay in.

FALLING ASLEEP IN in cars with strangers is supposed to be bad for you, but everyone tells you to fall asleep when you're travelling from one place to another. The only time I've known someone on the bus with me, we sat in different rows and didn't speak. I sleep best and longest alone. Quiet bed, quiet mind, quiet grave. Bury me in a way where no one can see. Lay me down in an ocean without fishes. When I sleep on the bus I do not dream, but when I sleep at home I don't dream either. So what's the point in looking for the horizon from the sweat-stained Plexiglas windows if you can't see them from the sweat-stained windows of your bedrooms? I guess we are never strange to the windows and people we have touched our faces against, so this is why we should sleep. It helps to have hope that a horizon is a place you can end up where no one will keep you from waking. Hope is a dream and a person too. Someone named Hope drives a bus. That bus is full of beds — you stand as you sleep. Once the dead skin of my cheek clings to another's by proxy of windowpane, their rest is my pillow, my rest will become another's. In old witchcraft, if you had skin or hair from someone, you could control that person. I know buses are safe zones of magical travel. I have to hope that there is something pure about them. Liminality, ya know? The place where the world is and isn't. I drift through upright positions of stasis to transit through myself quicker. I guess that's sleeping through the pain. Eventually we will all be healed or healthy — or maybe health is just the absence of pain. So when I die name me Healthy, name me Purity, Transit Belly Snore, Bumpy Road. Name me what you wish would wake you after a long road with no dreams, just gas stations for miles.

THE BODY SCAN machine at the airport
highlights only my crotch.

Sick —

which isn't exactly what I am
but hey, maybe my 2nd puberty means I'm gonna
grow up with a fire crotch.

Smoke blows through California and my friends
cannot breathe and I think of fire crotch
and maybe this is just
my body becoming
barren fields. Or this is some scene
in a movie where I part
my legs and my body
turns to ash.

All of the traveler kids knew
they were trans or ended up there.
It's a condition, like a sickness.

Cough cough — I'm gayer than I am happy,
than I ever will be.
It's a condition to pass
between the lines of things.

Cough cough — I sat alone on a 14-hour bus ride
and then asked about taking hormones,
my mouth merit badges.

(Does the teal of my Estradiol match my eyeliner?)

I do my makeup on the road, so does that make it
road rash?

The airport dude looks at the screen,
then at me, but mostly he stares
at my crotch and is like? *Where*

is your belt?

And I shrug, like? *Haven't you seen a trans femme*

hold themselves up?

Maybe this is why I don't like to fly,
why buses feel more like the vessel I could die
in. Planes are a wedgie against my
proverbial suicidal thoughts, whereas buses
are more interested in hearing me out
when I say I want to be worn
      in Death's mouth.
To be carried to the next city, pass
      a graveyard, and not
feel as if I am being carried into a grave.

But when am I going to be carried home first?

WHY DO ALL the words relating to my body
have to do with movement? Passing privilege,
transitioning. One thing, and then another thing.

I want more, but that doesn't mean I want to move.
I say I need to find a way to love myself, but that doesn't mean
I'm going to look for it too.

I was dysphoric, and then I started hormones.
Now I'm dysphoric with small tits.

I don't know how to write a poem that leaves [ ].

The going poem.
    The moving poem.
        Not the destination poem
      or   the journey poem, but
    the movement poem —
    the poem about transit,

about trans anything.

This is the single stall bathroom of road.

ONCE THERE WAS a dog and it was so
good at running and finding and
getting by and being in motion
that there was a bus by the same name.
A shitty bus, but capable.

I used to ask people what their
favorite thing about dogs was.
*Dogs just go. A dog can break its leg and
keep moving forward and think "well,
this is life now."*

A dog with a broken leg, lurching
forward.
A bus driving down a highway,
cargo doors open.

I WISH FOR sharper canines,
a mouth described as "a maw."
When I ask myself
what I'm transitioning toward,
my answer is blood.
I don't know
what type my blood is,
but I know that it is unusable.

What has blood done for me
that pills haven't?
What can I track down
that I can also smell?
What can find first — before
it becomes found?
I want to be like the wind,
        but not the wind.

Have the soft
underbrush of tall grass coat
my sides, form itself
into a blanket,
form itself a home around my jaw,
form itself a bandage
        across my sharpest edges,
        thin itself into floss or rasp.
Sharpen my teeth into something
that can tear open a fear.
Have a bark and a bite.

Have something to do
       other than slink into
the wind and be carried into the dirt.

Some of the first dogs mutated
after eating left-out garbage.

Maybe I was always feminine, or animal.
Maybe I was always eating scraps,

and so I thought myself scraping by.

I WANT TO see a well-fed trans person.
When I eat, I eat for show.

When I cook, it is because I am a spectacle —
something to watch, something to serve.

Being against your body is almost the same
as slow ideation. Caramelized onion suicide.

It takes time to learn to die if you want to be good at it.
I want to be good at it, be good at something.

When I say I want to see a well-fed trans person,
it is because I only know us as wanting creatures.

My flatmates in Hamburg ask me about English,
and I cook for them all. *Is it a lie when you tell someone*

the wrong thing on purpose, or is it a lie to be on the ground
flat, grave-like, neu-death, utopia of bones?

My friends get sad and I ask to make them a meal.
If they are full of sadness, or grief, why not also be full

of something else too? Maybe it can push out the bad,
maybe it can make space available for something better?

Find me a trans person who is well-fed on joy,
full of confidence, stuffed to the brim in a bed of roses,

one who can lie to themselves about their grief being over,
at least for now, at least until they are able to lie down again
and feel their bones rattle against the dirt. *You can say it's*
"cutlery" or "utensils," but utensils can mean a lot of things.

There are cooking utensils, eating utensils, gardening utensils.
Any set of tools can be a utensil for a specific purpose.

My bones are body utensils. My muscles are moving utensils —
specifically, my legs are moving utensils.

I have this hair which is part of my feminine utensil set.
It is extra filigree, like a knife with art nouveau inlaid on the handle.

My tattoos are detail work, filigree to the skin utensils.
Sometimes my heart is a sadness utensil, sometimes a love utensil,

but mostly an ache utensil. I ache into the things I make use of.
I ache over the food I cook. I ache over the body I have.

I ache over my anxieties, small meals only for myself.
When I say I see a well-fed trans person,

I mean I look into the mirror and
live longer, look like something so full

of movement that the sadness no longer stays as often —
it leaves holes when it is gone, an ache for an ache.

I TELL ANOTHER trans person
I feel most in my skin
in Greyhound bus terminals.
Neither of us talks
about what it means to only be seen in a liminal way —
to only be seen when we are in movement, between two points.

Let's talk about what liminal means.

Place without a name,
a home but not a door, a bird's nest, a bird, a feather.
When I mention liminal, I am speaking in a place without
time per se. It also has reference to being both in and out
of a boundary, which is a gender too.

Sorry, I dropped out twice so that means I don't need
to *actually* know definitions.
I went to college and learned I was a dumb bitch
so I left, which in turn solidified it.
There's a layer of privilege here.
When I die, they might debate what my true gender was
but no one will debate that I was in debt.

I don't have to know how to define anything, but I'm a poet
so I get to anyway.

Gender identity is the hallway in that book *House of Leaves*, I guess?
Like, yes, I have been in a closet, but also I am The Closet.

I tell another trans person about entering a Greyhound
terminal and being called *ma'am*, and how cursed
it is to be so aware of your nipples, and how feminized
they make you feel, and how in public you think this a bad thing
but wish so much for its normalcy to stay.

Shame is a chronic status for me.
It says something that I am so scared of being seen
that I feel gutted when I am.

Once, I told a partner that I wanted
to take hormones. I left on a Greyhound bus, blinked,
and then I was single. I have collectively spent over
one hundred hours on buses, and that's fine.

I take selfies in the only single stall bathroom
I ever feel safe in and   a bump
                                                in the road
makes me stay inside another 3 minutes
to get the perfect one.

OKAY FUCK IT, I'm On One.

For the purpose of being On One,
I am off the rails of myself.
        Loose cannon. Loose canon.

When I say I like travelling, I mean I like getaways.
Like getting away. Like, get away.

Yes, I'm transitioning,
but in a way that's cool and fun
        and not scary.

That's a joke.
It's actually scary to run away from my body,
because
            it's going to catch up before I know it.

The more I am witnessed,
the more I must be tangible
and therefore can be verifiably othered —
therefore I can be timeless.
I can be without timestamp; first I was,
then I repeated.

Witness me so I can witness me. I can't escape your distrust
of who I am as well as my own faith that I am at all.

Film me so I can go to you,
        so I can leave you.
        Film me so I can run from you.

WHEN I SAY I'm transitioning, I mean
first there was a boy and then
            there was nothing.

First there was rain, and now
there's just a dense fog.

Name it Gender —
something that flocks to the hills
and caves,
and a body,
and it roams and roams
until the first solid thing to hold it.

Meaning,

transitioning is my way
        of solidifying
                the vacuum of space.

When people say you can choose to be gay
but you can't choose your gender —
                        how sad for you.

If it was all a choice
you bet I wouldn't be cis or straight.

I'd be *fun*.

If it was a choice I'd be fun. But it's not,
                    so I'm just scared.
I love dogs, but I'm fearful of anything
                    that would eat me
were it not for mass-mutation.

Maybe that's what gender is.
Gender is a dog that barks all night.

I am flesh and blood,
something to keep you fed
        when you hunger.
        How big must a mouth
            be not to choke?

I know what to say, how not to think that
this too is a choice that we are all choosing to forget.

I CAN'T WAIT to be that dog-owning bitch
who defends my dog's pronouns.

I will teach my dog to defend my pronouns too.
Bitches gotta have each other's backs.

Cis men like to call cars she,
    boats she,
    cats she.

My dog that I spayed/neutered?
    that's my BOY
    that's my MAN
    that's my he.

If you own it, you can gender it they say.
Don't I own myself?

I will be the bitch in the dog park
wearing purple matte lipstick,
throwing a baton into the field
for my dog to chase after
so, when they return, I can use it
to thwack a TERF into the AstroTurf.

I won't paint my dog's nails,
but I will make sure they're healthy.
We might have to run
regardless of how safe it could be.

We might have to run away
even when we feel most powerful.

MAYBE I WAS always feminine, or animal.
Maybe I've had these sharp teeth and not bitten with them.

I think about the ways I have hounded myself
into my gender, into my body, out of my body,

and how I have bled because of what I tried to become.
Maybe I was feminine and animal, and now I am just ghost.

Men choose to confide in me
as a man — until I remind them that I don't exist.

They codify me masculine,
but I've turncoated our experiences.

Double agent for whom?
Watch out, I might tell on you.

Do you think the wind doesn't know
about what was built

to stop it? Do you think the wind
cared about the first wall?

I am like the wind, but not the wind.
The walls that confront me to disappear
into my gaits — into my gates.

I'm going to live in the exact way the brain tricks you
into seeing something you wouldn't believe.

I will be something a brain will forget rather
        than make sense of.

I am something the brain would rather forget
        than make sense of.

Do you ever hear a voice
call your name in a crowd,
only for no one to be there
        when you look?

That was me
and all the ways I wish I was looked for.

I'M TRYING TO do this thing where I get my license, which means one day I'll separate myself from the bench of a bus station and graduate into sleeping in the backseat of a car I own. I used to think I knew the best places to sleep in Union Station, but now I know the best place is just the one that carries you, keeps you going, allows you to pass between travels. It is in those chairs that we can find respite, because what else is there to find in the crevice of someone else's warmth? If spending the night in a different state qualifies as having lived there, then I have lived in many. When I get a car, I will never wear pants again and no one can stop me. No one can look at and judge me either, which is the actual goal. But here we are: me, my skirt on with sweat coating my thighs, two kissing hairless cats, and you, sprawled with one leg in the aisle, and the other reaching for the window, hoping to push me out of the way and into the road. I think it would be nice to die in a desert. Joke: dissociative identity disorder was first used in 1993.

Joke: it takes about a week after travelling
to remember who I am or that I am in
my body, or that this body travelled
and the mind did too. There are worse
tactics for keeping yourself alive, but
I am that bitch.

MARTA TALKS TO me about the "possibility" of the big happiness
that comes with travel, but also the innumerable smaller possibilities.

Like, yes, it would be ideal to get mountains and tall trees,
but there is also joblessness and no pets allowed and allergies.

I am a series of possibilities – but so far I am not a possibility
who also gets a dog. Just a mid-tier femme who can't do eyeliner very well.

I am the possibility of good eyeliner but like, not.

The possible outcome of taking a bus is sitting alone, but usually you aren't;
you sit with varying levels of discomfort.

Once, on a bus from Baton Rouge to New Orleans, some man
kept grunting and huffing and I thought about how easy it would be
      for him to end me.

Not in an *end me please* kind of melancholy lust drive,
but in the sense that I could die in a state where no one knows me.

Not even by names I have long since thrown out the window.

The possible outcome of starting HRT is to be alone. But being alone
by not starting it, or by starting it and later ending it, is also a possibility.

I do not think people who were close to me left because of hormones.
It was because they realized I was going to be a bitch forever.

Where I'm trying to go, me being a bitch is not a possibility
but a definitive fixed point.

There's no anxiety in this always-conflict.
There's a surplus of it in the forever-death drive,
      in the idea of mountains::
      in the idea of mounted::
      in the idea of my mouth, I carry pills

and varying levels of discomfort.

AS A TRAVELLING artist, returning is a question on the constant-past.
I'd love to believe that a thing is as I left it, just for once.
But that never happens. Things are constantly in motion.

I leave home and return
home, but it's different.

I once left home and returned to a friend butt-ass
in my bed with a stranger, so I left again. Returned again
to the same thing, but different: their ghostly sex stains.

Leave home and a bed frame. Return to a pile of wood,
which seems like a good metaphor for broken
cycles or upbringings. But there's only so much absence
one can take, even if it makes the space seem that much bigger.

People ask me how places were, not how I am,
like there's still travelling in this body.
I got a lot of mileage in these bones still.

Yes, I do mean it when I say it was fine,
the same as when I say I am also fine.

It's like asking how I wear my dysmorphia
differently between Thursday and Friday.

Casual Friday dysmorphia is me at work shaking cocktails
because it makes what little breasts I have feel like True Breasts.

A body of movements breaking and rebuilding.
The ghost movement of my body as a pleasurable sight.

I won't say that I haven't stained the rooms
of lovers with my absence, because I can't.

My body moves toward what magnetizes it, and I let it.
It took me too long to learn the best way to love myself.

It's taking me too long to learn the best way to love myself,
but I'll keep trying
                    trying
                    trying
                    trying
                    trying
                    trying
                    trying
                    trying
                    tiring
                    trying
                    trying
                    trying
                    tiring
                    trying
                    trying
                    tiring
                    trying
                    tiring

SEX HAS NEVER been a language I could understand, but I have learned to get by with it, have cut myself loose out of bear traps with it. I have fucked my way into the safety of a bed frame away from home, and then fucked my way out of it too. There are pictures of me on the kitchen island between the room I came out in and the mattress on the floor of the living room where a once-lover called for the ghost of my masculinity to fuck the me out of me and into them. Exorcise the male so it could possess theirs. I know how to ask for help in sex, how to ask to be seen, to see myself. Lovers have eaten my ears, my eyes, my tongue, but no one can stomach my stomach — it's so full of acid I'd corrode the floorboards with my sweat. There are colonies of carpenter bees in the buildings I've biled in, and I do not apologize for their work. It's taken me too long to grow and hear my voice again. I don't know what help sounds like from a mouth not on my throat, but I know that I beg for it to mask what comes next — what I hope comes next. Teeth, and then an end I don't clean myself up out of.

MAYBE I WAS never feminine, or animal.
Maybe I need to learn that wanting something

into existence is not creation, just want.

I am want for womanhood as I am want for maleness,
or for how I want for animalia again, or for the first time.

The body wants for air forever, and then it doesn't.
The body wants for rest in small doses, and then it indulges.

The body wants for movement, and then stations itself around it.
The body wants for itself until it rejects itself.

I don't want to be a body someone can identify
after death. But if I am found, make me myself.

Not feminine, or animal, or masculine, or even corporeal.
When I say I want to be like the wind, but not the wind,

I mean I hope to move against anything
that could possibly grasp me — and refuse it.

Refusal is as much my gender as it is all gender.
It is the one I have always lived with.

First there was a body with teeth and they got worse,
so they wished themselves sharper.

Then from sharpness the body reduced its maw into nothing.
And what is nothing but an amount of water? So the body synthesized.

The body waits for things to be okay, even when they won't be.
The want for things doesn't end, so why should I stop wanting

for a body that is anything but what it is? Or to stop
wanting for anything altogether? By which I mean, to become death.

THIS ISN'T JUST about me anymore.
This is about the movement of all bodies.
This can't just be about me anymore, rather —
there is so much more at stake than myself.

The body of the government polices
the body of the community, which in turn
makes the communities and those in them
bodies marginalized by the government.
There are borders within borders.

Who, when they make it on
the bus, does so with a fear
they won't make their destination?
Gendered bodies, Black bodies, bodies of color, disabled bodies,
queer bodies. Bodies against the government.

The body of the government is ruled
by the body of money, which is true even if it isn't.
Men buy their way into others' safety and travel through
the poverty of the world, creating the poverty of the world.

My friend tells me that prisons should be abolished —
                              and I agree.
My friend tells me that everyone in prison should be rehabilitated —
                              and I agree.
My friend tells me that all of the police, and the guards, and the army
should put into the prisons for twenty years after they are abolished —
                              and I cannot agree.

If it isn't about power, then what?
Replacing the incarcerated people with those who upheld the system
will only make prisons continue. If they are still open,
what is to stop someone from trying to use them, to profit from them?

Money moves through the
body of people, and all there
is for me to grasp is myself. I
am grateful to have the means
to become myself, grateful
to have the ability to move
forward, to open up. The body
of genders is one of expenses.
Why do you think there
are so many anti-capitalist
trans persons? My body, my
gender, my movement, is
against borders, against
prisons, against their
accomplices: money, power,
civility. I'm told not to get
off the train or bus between
Hamburg and Berlin, that it's
white supremacist territory,
but also that it is beautiful.

There is nothing beautiful about territory run by white supremacy.
There is nothing beautiful about having to closet yourself
to survive a stint of transit. There is beauty in surviving,
but it is a type of beauty that is fleeting and fixed.

Once I entered a room feminine and felt wonderful.
Before, I entered a room hunted and felt prey. But
got to be prey because I was pretty, so I should feel lucky.

Once, I had a job that let me be who I am.
Then the job showed me if someone assaulted me
I would be at fault for bringing that upon myself.
How lucky I would have to be to attract death.

Yet, that's all we do as trans persons —
move from fixed point to fixed point of safety
until our ability to reach is diminished by something
someone would call   luck.

> The movement that
> runs tandem with
> containment is
> movement that will
> never allow me to be
> trans. The lawless
> state of transit has
> been both haven and
> prison. The movement
> from fixed point of
> safety doesn't run on
> asphalt, but through
> time. This fixed point
> of clarity will be met
> with an abstract point
> of confusion.

I want to be on a bus or a train that takes me
to a fixed point rooted in persons.
I want to find the place
where the body of genders
becomes itself an abstract

point of clarity.
      Take me there, Greyhound.
      Take me there, Amtrak.
      Take me there, roads.

MAGPIE WRITES ABOUT the immortal with pity, and there lies some conflict. If the immortal are imbued with skepticism, anxiety, and thanatophobia, then the immortal would probably be transphobic. A Bible Belt of elves. I know that to get anywhere brings about change and, as I write this, getting anywhere means a road to ride upon. If the road means mitigating danger, then the unmoving immortal would run parallel to an unmoving trans identity, wouldn't it?

As a kid, I believed in dragons and elves and magic.
What is more interesting than a world where death
is not the scariest thing, but rather a welcomed end to a fully lived life?

We are dying.

I say this in the overarching We to claim everyone in this,
but also because We as in the Trans-We are dying.
More specifically, We are being killed
by the unmoving, skeptic, anxious, the immortal.

When I say someone who cannot die would be transphobic, I mean to say death is the last transition goal I have. There was a beginning step (I started accepting myself), and there is an end step (getting to live long enough to have a choice when and how I die). The immortal do not care about my transition

goals because the immortal would consider
transitioning as a way to place myself farther
toward Thanatos. If I can't control how I die,
at least I want to know how to feel good about
it.

I'm mitigating the danger I'm putting myself into by transitioning.

Were I to reject myself, I would lean
further into "taking myself out."
I used to want to become the immortal —
if I could never die, I would figure out
         why I was always so sad.
         I started transitioning, and did.
The ephemeral immortal are full of fear of change.
Change that repositions yourself closer to a kind of death
you might not have as much awareness of.

When We say trans people are braver
than any person serving in any military,
We mean to say that the presence of death
in our lives is ever-rotating and changing.
We must grin and scream at danger.
The alternative is an absence of grinning,
                            of only screaming.

I wear a seatbelt, I drive at reasonable speeds. But I won't get anywhere if I don't get on the road.

And so the road is where I go.
If the seatbelt of being trans is passing,

then passing is the horizon.
Sometimes the buses, trains,
bicycles, trams, planes, legs
I use lead me toward it —
and at other times I try to get away from it.

The difficulty is that, on a circular planet
(and through this I know the planet is circular),
the horizon shifts to wherever We are looking.

There is always a part of me trying
to mitigate my transness by passing,
or being on the line of the horizon
standing in front of a sun and the immortal
looking toward me but only seeing brightness.
Seeing something that they can only name in essence.

HOMESICKNESS IS A disease without reason.
I have found cures in the flat Canada Dry,
in the seafood seasoning, in the guilt.

I am away and I am homesick for comfort.
Homesick for something to hold me, or to be held.
Homesick for my dysphoria, for my depression.

I crave caves that know my names,
because I like to know that I am known.
Echo myself into existence, eon after Aeon.

                    When I'm out in the city,
I don't speak unless spoken to. Even then,
my mouth is a flood of languages I can't recognize.

I am homesick for singularity. Singularity at the hand
of being the Other. There is a person, and then there
is me: next to them, but not them.

At times when people see me and not my body
as I see it, they make me homesick to be uncomfortable,
because it's something I know how to be.

I don't know how to be the agender femme
and also to be believed as one. I don't know
so much about myself, as no one taught me.

My flatmate sees me sick with grief and
they bring me a plate of strawberries.
These cure homesickness.

And they do, and I am grateful —
not for the berries (though they are delicious),
but for the comfort of being held as I am.

To be treated for my Otherness as an Other.
There are languages, and then there is my mouth.
There is my mouth. There is my mouth and its

gaping jaw as I swallow what I can of this moment.
There is this depression and this dysphoria,
and there is me, between them.

I need to learn myself whole as having their hands,
and straying from them. I want to position myself
in my skin, and say my skin is my home.

One day I will be homesick for my body,
for a name that is no longer my name;
they are parts of me only I own the memory of.

Tears for my names as they move from my skin.
Tears for my skin as I blot it with ink.
Tears for the page and its once-empty kingdom,

so full of promise and nothing. I used to say
I would never get words tattooed on me.
Well, guess what bitch.

I've never been the reliable narrator, but
I have always been on the side of the truth
that keeps going. If you hold the white paper

against the white desk, the desk becomes the paper as
the paper makes itself the desk. There are no borders
in identity poetics (something I want to say but can't).

There are lines that divide us into smaller communities,
and then there is everyone who doesn't fit.
The Island of Misfit Bodies.

In this trans novel, a spirit travels to a
seemingly untouched place. An island that
looks nearly like everywhere at once. Here
is the Space Needle State Empire Building.
Here, the spirit will see bodies like our
bodies, and poltergeists withering. It is the
place the dead who have come back in the
form of a body-snatch go when they get into
a body they can't remove again. Born-again
into the wrong body. This spirit will try to
help, but there is nothing our protagonist
will do. There is a pitch for a sequel that
teases how spirits can switch and land in a
body that is more their idealized identity,
but it is in publishing purgatory. Later, the
author will reflect and say it's unrealistic. A
book about people being unhappy because of
how the world makes them see themselves just
doesn't speak to a market where not everyone
examines their gender perception.

I have 20/20 Gender Vision.

I have an acute awareness of how my body moves
without my wanting. This blood travels
when I ask it not to, in movement

against me. My blood is against my stopping it.
My blood is homesick for the me that moves
when it does, that runs to the problem of my identity.

I dive into dysphoria, and I miss the water.
The air is a pool that carries my body —   a spirit
looking for a body that carries it best.

That body is my body though,
        and I know this. It is the   True Comfort.
        It isn't North, but   True North.
I am homesick for a version of myself in the future

where the moving continues,
but I have to run to get there, or else
I might miss
        myself seeing who I am first.

MAYBE I WAS never feminine, or animal.
Never wind, or like the wind,
but in the wind and near the wind.

Let it be known that the wind
is a sovereign identity, that anything with a curve
can be feminine if they wish it first.

Name an animal defined by its sharpest points,
and I can show you a shape a man has claimed.
I used to be such a taken body.

Now I take my body into my arms each night,
unlike how one takes a lover: my arms, the night.
My arms: the moon, the horizon, eclipsed.

I was never feminine or animal,
but I would like to be — and is that too much?
Maybe I was never feminine or animal, but

I was always too much, and that's why
want flows out my mouth, a gust of wind —
never wind or like the wind, but making it.

In a dream I use a pendulum to talk to the dead,
and in a dream I am again overwhelmed when the dead,
or anyone, responds to my voice.

Let it be known that my body is a sovereign state.
Let it be known that anything that moves is on a swivel.
Let me know how to echo back into my body, a pendulum

at first away from myself, and then back again.

LET'S SAY FOR argument's sake that we are a body made of bodies.
A body of water is made of a body of wetness, sibling to a cloud —
which is also a body made of wetness.

The body of a body is also made up of wetness, but the wetness of the body
is made up of smaller bodies: molecules and microbes.
One could say that the human body is made up of small non-human bodies.

The body of being alive is the body of energies. The body of energies
is the body of confusion. Everyone is trying so hard to figure out
why we are alive. It would be a shame to find out, probably.

If the body of a cisgender person is made up of non-human bodies,
how do we know the non-human genders in the body are also cisgender?
Maybe born in the wrong body is a microbial standpoint.

The body of transgender persons is a body of water, a body of molecules,
a body of clouds, a body of energies, a body of confusion. The non-human
bodies are the powerhouse of the cell. The cell being either the person
        or the prison.

The body opposite of water is the body of fire — one made up of kindling.
The body of kindling is made up of whatever catches. The body of fire
is a part of the body of smoke and steam, and therefore cousin to
        the body of a cloud.

The non-human parts of cis bodies are related to the non-human parts
        of trans bodies.
Both bodies bleed similarly enough, but one body catches easier.
        The body of the cis

is a part of the body of water — the body of the trans is part of the body
of fire and of water.

If you can light water on fire, it's better to say it's oil.
If you feel heat, you say *fire*. If you feel damp, say *rain*. But for both,
you don't say much at all. The body of the trans does the saying.

The body of the saying is what makes up the body of the scream.
The body of the snitch is cousin, the body of the silence is opposite
and also adjacent.

If the body of the trans is the body on fire, the non-human parts of the body
burn into the body of noises, into the body of ash.
Maybe the microbial parts of us were born into the wrong human body.

If the body of a pyre is the body of kindling, the kindling
is part of the body of a forest, parent body to the body of trees.
Making it also the parent body to the body of a faggot.

Queer and trans bodies are part of the body of a faggot,
part of the body of a forest, bodies of the earth.
Buried bodies are the human parts of a non-human body.

If a faggot is representative as a bundle bound for a pyre,
upon which to throw atypically presenting persons,
then the faggot also symbolizes that which is used
to burn the witches and noisemakers and spiritualists.

For the purpose of the metaphor, assimilating into death machines
is what the cis want even if they don't want us.

An enlisted queer can be a dead queer. A queer in the police
knows where to find the rest. A queer politician is brainwashed.

So many trans and gender nonconforming persons in my life
are becoming witches, herbalists, noisemakers, spiritualists.
It only makes sense to operate in secrecy when we already do.
The webcams are watching. We snitch on ourselves in our search
        for community.

If one queer person is used to destroy another queer person,
how can we have faith in each other to not eat each other alive?
I want to be the bigger bitch, but we have been hurt so much.
Trust is an empty spell. It's hard to cast it when there's not even us
        to catch us.

The cis want this. The heteros want this. If you can
get your enemy to destroy itself, what's the point in hate, then?
I never want to see my rapist again, but I will not be the pyre, or on the pyre,
if I can help it. What is the point of destroying
                        that which wants to destroy us?

A trans person in power is a good thing, and that's all I should feel.
But even still I fear so much, where our information goes.
I fear the day when a trans census is used to round us up.
I've said before that privatized gays code-break queerness;
if I can look it up on the internet, it isn't a safety I can have.

The moving queer parts of the universe slide in and out of our sharpnesses.
I worry so much for young noisemakers. Who will they accidentally
        snitch to?
I worry so much for the elders who got to become elders.

I am sorry you have to watch us fight to make mistakes your friends died for.

If the faggot is a pyre, and the medium is placed above it
        — on fire —
then why not burn everything down?
Why not run from the flames
into the buildings they built
to keep the queers out?

I dream of movement for all.
I dream of a body that breaks and runs anyway.
We read about protagonists and antagonists who
are damaged beyond themselves —
and still they fight on,
so valiant or so terrifying.
I dream of a body of genders
that is valiantly terrifying.
I dream of a body of genders
that saves as it slaughters.
I dream of a body of genders
shapeless as all hounds are shapeless.
I dream of a body of genders
that fights until it cannot,
        and then continues.
That runs until it is wounded —
        and then keeps going.

There is nothing holding us back
from building a community of our best selves
but our worst selves —
        a self we all have.

There is nothing that can kill us
that hasn't already.
The slow lurch toward hell is paved
with the bones of dead queers.
Hell itself is the bodies of those against us
that we dragged to the mouth and let fall in.
I dream of the movement of bodies
    like ocean currents
    forever breaking.

IF THIS IS a poem about moving, where is it
going? Where is it going to take us if not
away from something else? The movement
asks us where we would like to be, and we go.
But what do we need to leave behind to get
there? What sacrificial offerings do we leave
behind to transit?

> I leave safety in tiny
> pockets of winter
> coats of the country.

> If I can remember an
> address and get to a
> city, I can be someone
> who continues to
> travel, rather than
> stops, indefinitely.

If there is a way to be among company, there
is a way to become a part of a larger whole,
wholly myself and wholly the group. I want
to be a part of the end-machine that stops
the movement of war.

When we talk about movement, what the writer, the reader,
the poem, the story, the article, the conversation must recognize
movement that happens without our urgency —
  in fact, regardless of our urgency or agency.
      The movement of militarization.
      The movement of police.
      The movement of borders.
      The movement of bodies.

If we can get to a place where someone knows our names,
that does not mean safety, always. The borders are snakes.
The police and the military are snakes. The government is snakes.
If you watch the movement of enough of them in a row,
you see the movement of a river. Life is a constant crossing
of water, of rivers, of snake nests.
We sacrifice so much to become safe
in a world that is increasingly against our safety.

When we talk about bodies, it's important to point out
that not all bodies are allowed to move.
Like chess, the ones in the highest positions of power
move the most, but some still only move within restrictions.
    I change my name
but everything you would find to identify my body stays the same.
I am white and that means I'm more likely to be alive, if I am found.
Within gender there is sacrifice. There are one million scales
we push and pull sand from. I am ashamed of the safety
I've asked for despite myself, in spite of my gender.
My body and my gender sacrifice less
so that I can move in this body, in this country,
in the ways that I can,
and for that I am thankful.

When we talk about war, we have to talk about complicit movement.
    If we have the opportunity to stand against nationalism,
        do.
    If we have the opportunity to stand against prisons,
        do.
    If we have the opportunity to stand against borders,
        do.

The body of a border is against the movement
of diverging selves, against the ability to be oneself and be alive.

If the poem is about movement, the
poem recognizes when not to move.
If the poem must move, it moves in
tandem with bodies moving for other
bodies. I move to the world where
snakes are solely snakes, by which I
mean to a world against the police,
   against prison,
   against borders.
I move to a world of snakes. What
was nature should return to it.
    When I am dead,
transition my body into the earth. Use
my bones against power, use my hair
against power, move my body against
what I am against, what is against me,
what helped me die how I lived, how
so many do,
    looking for safety.

57

I'VE BEEN GOING about this all wrong.
Maybe I wasn't, and then I was.
I wasn't what I wanted to be,
until I wanted to be that way, and then I was.
Salmon are against the stream,
but they are the stream.
Does that make the salmon a current too?
What qualifies something as "the quo"?
There must be some things
that are like the quo, but not the quo.
If I was never feminine,
what was I but myself?
If I was never animal,
what was I but alive and moving?
I felt like the absence of a worthy identity.
And, in that moment, I felt feminine.
Maybe, to be specific, I was never femme
but always animal, always craving
something to last a lifetime,
for something to go on forever.
Maybe my trans is a layer cake:
first the world called it Boy
and my body responded Butch
but my heart still hopes for Femme.
I could never be feminine without also being animal.
Animalia runs through my genders
more than anything else, blows a gust
against my blood.
   Abrasion heart.

When I say I want to be like the wind
but not the wind, this is what I mean:
        timeless,
            forever-sprawling touch,
                without position,
without anything to identify it
            but its presence.
Just like when I say the salmon
are against the stream
but a part of it too,
the salmon and the stream
beat against each other
forever into animalia.

Maybe I've been going about this all wrong.
Rather than searching for something that lasts,
I've been hoping to become what ends.
Death is the forever I hope my gender becomes,
and I weep because of it.

                    Never Ending Story of Bones.
I never want to exist in a story
with a clean ending,   so I won't.
Maybe I was never Always, and always Never.
Always Timeless, never Timemore,
never not a current, always current,
an always-going, never recorded.
If the human body regenerates cells
so every decade or so, the outside me
is one that has never seen the sun.

Maybe I'm an outlier.
Rather than getting to stay my size forever,
my gender is always decaying;
a literal lifetime.

I LEAVE MY body, and return to it the same, but different.
Each time it prisms back onto me.

Show me who I mirror, Mirror.
That's the point, right? To be defined
by the person people reflect into you.

If you know me as a frame, you can call me Mirror.
If you walk through me, name me Door.
Refract me into what space you need me to fit,
and I will stay there until I am moved again.

At times, this body stays still and the world
shifts around me; oil to water, blood to oil.
In a life, I ran cross country. Picture me:

shorts and sweat and blotched skin.
Define me by the identities that make sense:
I was young and assumed

how this all-of-me lived.
I ran with a group of myselves.
Let's name a group of people your age "a collection";

let's call an action "an item"; let's say
I was left and so I must be "lost."
Running in a group is called "a purpose."

So, when I was left behind, I became "an effort."
It is no effort to figure out who I am

without knowing how I have lived,
without knowing how I have ended.

Ending defined by yelling.
Ending defined by shatter.
If my life is framed by whoever looks at it,

what would I build if not a place where I can hide?
If a person is described by what they have
reflected into them,

what can I find in myself if I prism?
A life as bad skin.
A life as bad hair.

A life as square jaw, square shoulders,
boxes of bodies with no room in storage.
I was left to my own devices,

so I ran eight miles on my own until
a man yelled me into light beams because he lost
me. I stopped doing cross country,

but I still run away from what hurts me most.
The track coach said the pole vaulters were suicidal,
which is true but not in the way he joked.

A prism defined by what stays inside of it,
a hunger defined by what it needs to quell,
a wind emptied into the esophagus of me.

If someone wants to define me by what I refract,
then prism me into infrareds,
prison me out of this gender,

prism me into something framed by a horizon —
something unreachable, where
the yells are named whispers,

and the foot fall is followed by itself
until the horizon becomes itself a comforter,
and the sun tucks the body into bed around it.

🐎 ACKNOWLEDGMENTS 🐎

This project started in the same way it was written: at the center finding its way to the edges. *Greyhound* would not be possible if not for the arms that have caught me between travels. I have a lot of people to thank, but I want to thank MYSELF first. My relationship with myself has never been a stable one, but the trust I've been able to put on myself to get from one point and then another is invaluable. There are so many people and experiences I wouldn't have accrued if not for the initial trust that if I put my foot forward I'll find stable ground in time. Coming back at the center of myself has always been a point of contention, but I am thankful.

GREYHOUND, AMTRAK, BOLTBUS, FLIXBUS, MEGABUS, MARC TRAINS, BICYCLES, SKATEBOARDS, CARPOOLS, ETC., thank you. This poem was birthed in motion. This book is the static home it lives in, but the voice will always be between destinations. Thank you to PHOENIX, OAKLAND, TORONTO, VANCOUVER, MONTREAL, BATON ROUGE, JEMEZ SPRINGS, NEW YORK CITY, WASSAIC, HAMBURG, and RICHMOND. Without these cities where I've had to place myself, where I've been found, and where I've been accepted, I doubt that I would get the clarity needed to write this. Special thanks to IO, to DESIREE and BRYAN, to CLEMENTINE, to ASHLEY, NAVID, MARCELLA, to EVA, and to E: you are all cities of people as well. Thank you for allowing me to squat in your hearts.

MARTA, there would be no direction were it not for your journeys to drive me to take my own. The grand possibility of always choosing yourself, of letting yourself feel whatever it is you are feeling, and of knowing when to keep going — I learned all of this from you.

VILLA MAGDELENA K. Without the acceptance and stay in this artist-in-residence program, I don't think I'd have a recollection for what "home" looks like to me, for where my body lives, and for what I want to make it look like when it holds others. I reference my time in Hamburg in this poem as one of remembrance because it reminded me of why I was writing this poem to begin with. This piece is not a poem just for moving myself, but was always meant for the communities that choose to hold me and in which I found myself. Thank you NINA, LAURA, ANDREW, SHIRIN, and ENO.

NEON, without knowing you I would not have known the shape and binds my body makes. You have always been at the intersection of movement and motion that I wish to frequent.

THE WASSAIC PROJECT. My time at the end of the Metro North train was short but incredibly informative in being able to translate the movement of this piece. Spending time collaborating with artists of all mediums is wildly fulfilling, and showed me better and broader ways of turning this poem and my writing in general into conversations rather than statements. WILL, SIEL, EVE, BOWIE, JEFF, TARA. Thank you for your acceptance of my work in the broader conversation of art. JANET, LAUREN, STEFFI, MARLO, ANDY, PATTI, SOPHIE. It's a joy to know that we have met, and that my art is changed for it. JULIA, I am doubtful I will ever discard the notes you took on my work. To know you've spent time there is enough to continue. Without knowing you, NICOLE, I don't think I'd have ever thought of my work being welcome outside the page or the stage. Who would have thought the trajectory of our lives would bring us from acquaintances, to coworkers, to co-residents, and (to me) an inspiration.

The eyes that poured over my work and helped set the course that it continued on to this point. My ferrymen. My shipmates. LIZ, HANNAH, J. BAILEY, ERIN, SYDNEY. I know how to move, but with your help the movement has a semblance of order and direction. Thank you.

In an argument against direction though, the journey would have nowhere to go if not toward chaos. If there was a club in my heart, I would find you there. That energy kept things in motion as well. REBECCA, ANDREA, LIX, thank you.

All of this to say that, without a place to return to, there would be no poem. There is nothing I could say to capture all of the thanks I could give to BALTIMORE CITY, but here is an attempt. There's plenty of opportunity in any direction, but really why would I want to go anywhere else when I live here? It's never been hard to leave the city because there truly is nothing like coming back to a place that you know fully and completely to be a home to you. I wanted to echo that feeling most of all in this poem, but I know it falls short. Thank you to the community of SPOKEN WORD POETS, SLAMMERS, and PERFORMANCE ARTISTS here for shepherding me to where I am and for instilling the pride I need to have in my own work. SLANGSTON, JACOB, BRION, KENNETH, SUMAIYAH, KHALID, MECCA, and GRIM. Thank you to the MUSICIANS and ARTISTS here that make me proud to be a part of the same cohort. Thank you to the RESTAURANTS I've worked in, the CAFÉS I've frequented, the PARKS and the SIDEWALKS, the ROOFTOPS and the PORCHES.

Thank you, with the most sincerity I can muster, to MICHAEL and SARAH. Were it not for the two of you, I wouldn't know how to make my body move as it does and I wouldn't have the trust to know that whoever is moving with me will catch me as I arrive.

Thank you to the people that make this city a home to me. AMY, DREW, KIRSTY, SAM, ABBY, HEATHER, KELLY. A location is a place, but the people who live there make it a home.

Greyhound of course would not be in the form it takes today without the trust and hands of NOEMI PRESS. Without the direction of DIANA, CARMEN, and SARAH, it would simply still be in motion. But it is with as much thanks as I can muster that the legs it has have arrived here, in a way I couldn't imagine.

Pieces of the poem have found homes throughout the years in ANOMALY, BALTIMORE BEAT, BELTWAY QUARTERLY, HOBART, PEACH MAG, THE PURITAN, and WYVERN LIT.

Thank you to JOE. This is a poem that, more than anything, I wish for you to read. Your drive and your spirit helped me write it. Rest easy.

PHOTO BY EMMA JOHNSON

AEON GINSBERG is a trans feminine agender writer and performer from Baltimore City, MD, where they live and work as a bartender. They are the author of two chapbooks, *Until The Cows Come Home* (Elation Press, 2016) and *Love/Loathe/Lathe* (Nostrovia! Press, 2017). They are a Taurus, and a bitch.